DECODING BUSINESS EQUATION

A Beginners Guide on How to Build Simple Home Business and Some Small
Home Business Ideas

By Advocate ABHISHEK GOKHALE

Copyright © 2020 Author Name Abhishek Gokhale

All rights reserved.

ISBN: 9798644290611

DEDICATION

This book is firstly and primarily dedicated to my very supportive readers and special dedication to my family and to all my friends without which this book won't have been written. I also dedicate this book to the laborers who motivated me to write this book and generate charity for them; lastly I am dedicating this book to my beloved nephew Rigved who is an avid reader and my biggest motivator.

CONTENTS

ACKNOWLEDGMENTS

Thank you firstly to Amazon for giving me the opportunity for publishing the book and the almighty god who has given me a healthy mind and body to write this book. I also want to thank the person under who guidance and tips I was able to write this book. To all the people, friends and family members who I met and thru their experience I was able to reproduce the same in this book.

INTRODUCTION

The world has changed and now after lockdown the world won't remain the same. There is a greater possibility that many of you would be losing your job and getting a new job in some company would be difficult. Like you I was also in the corporate vicious circle till the time I realize the inner potential within myself and that motivated me to leave the corporate field and be self-dependent. As you all know the great English proverb "Necessity is the mother of invention" and I want you to get out from your comfort zone and comprehend the inner potential within yourself, don't wait for the time you will lose anything and start something on your own from today itself. I am writing this book because there is a greater chance for you to flourish in your business once the lock down is over as there won't be a competition if you try and build up your small business right from your home without any investment right now when you have plenty of time in your hand.

Business or business ideas which I am sharing with you in this book are the day to day chores which you must be doing but really won't be aware about the potential earning capacity underlying in the daily chorus which you are doing. In this book no only I would be sharing the business ideas but also how you can identify and judge whether the business idea which you have chosen is right for you and whether you would be profiting with those business idea.

My Simple Workable Business ideas from home are tried and tested and even though it might not give you a great income at the beginning but at least will build up an inner potential in you to do something on your own and not to depend on any third party to support yourself. Once the idea of self-dependency inculcates within you and you build a habit of surviving on your own you will see the world in completely different sense without any boundaries and without any deadlines or pressure.

Why I am giving these business ideas is to develop a habit of surviving on your own and build a legacy or an intellectual property for your children so that they don't have to worry on finding a job or doing what the crowd in general is doing.

Lastly my main intention and reason for writing this book is to motivate you to do something on your own and realize the inner infinity potential within yourself and to understand that each and every one of you who is reading this book has tremendous potential within yourself and all you need to do is identify it and make the dreams come true. Many people will fail in the attempt to start their own business but the main idea is to learn from those failure and then build a business which will give you a greater independence and sense inner satisfaction which cannot be attain by doing a mere job or earning a monthly salary working for someone. My idea with this book is to inculcate a habit of self-realization self-dependency and self-motivation with the business which you would be building by reading this book.

This book also contains how to identify the business which is suitable for you as well as Simple business ideas which can be done without any investments.

CHAPTER 1

HOW TO IDENTIFY THE BUSINESS?

When there are so many businesses already running around you, it is a very good question to ask on how to identify a business which would be suitable for you. The idea behind identifying the business is very simple first of we have to understand and analyse ourselves the potential which we have and things which we can do easily. There might be something's which you are very good at and there might be some skills which you have in-built which you have not explored. Everyone is unique and the world is full of unique people some people have developed skills unknowingly by doing the same things repeatedly; you have to identify whether you have those skills inside you which can be put a potential use. Every household in a family there a member who has such a kind of skills and unknowingly he or she has developed those skills which they don't realize, to know these skills you have to give yourself time and identify within yourself which is that skill in which you are very good at, once you have identified the skill that very skill itself can be turned in a great business idea without any investment. *Abraham Lincoln was quoted as saying "Give me six hours to chop down a tree and I will spend the first four sharpening the axe"* this great quote by the great leader has a deep meaning and that what I am talking about a Skill which has been developed within yourself by doing a thing continuously it might be exercising regularly, reading, cooking, baking, event planning, blogging, etc it could be anything.

Here I would like to quote a story of my very close friend who has very good voice suitable for public speaking and had built a habit or a skill of talking in public or group of friends and without even knowing he had developed a skill of good public speaking which he was unaware of. Over the years after completing his graduation he was busy working in a private firm doing a 9:00 to 5:00 without realizing the true potential within him and many years he was struggling with his job switching over from one company to another and on top of that no happy in what he was doing. After many years of struggle when he was free from his financial liabilities he quit his job and started giving lectures in private colleges suddenly he realize his true potential within himself which he was unaware off for so many years. Time passed by and now he is successful public speaker and delivering lectures in many colleges and has his own institute of public speaking. My friend owing to the skill is very successful in his own field and on top of that is enjoying whatever he is doing at his leisure and comfort.

The Skill even though is an important factor of starting or identifying a business is not the only thing which can help you to identify the business there are many other things which one can utilize to identify the business. The point is to identify which business to start and to start such a business which will enable to achieve a long term goal and not to start something which you get bored off easily and give up in between.

My idea to tell you to start a business of your own interest is to keep you continuing to do the business even if you are not earning in initial phase as it will keep you are interest alive and to develop an identity of your own.

The idea to break the chain of monotonously working for somebody else and create your own future with your own hands, once you develop the habit of surviving without working for someone the life would be of greater meaning for you, the autonomy you get from the same would be limitless, this will enable to put in your creativity and your ideas and to enable it to eventually become a successful business opportunity for you.

There are thousands of business which are unexplored and with your potential and identifying those opportunities by clearing the clutter of your mind and deeply thinking on the ideas which can enable to start your business you can and achieve a business model suitable for you at the comfort of your home. The idea behind is to give a positive approach to your thoughts unclutter your mind and give your thoughts a meaningful way a thinking which is focused one and an approach which is of long term.

To get a focused thinking and approach you have to meditate or deeply think on the aspects which make you an individual, what are the good and the bad things in you and what make you as an individual. What are your strengths and playing with your strengths is what will make your business a successful one. As I said earlier in the quote if you want to cut a tree in 6 hours you have to sharpen your axe for 4 hours, it simple means to start a business you need to first study on the opportunities and the various other aspects of business and then venture rather than just simply in a haphazard way enter into the business and then fail. Failure is good learning when you are entering a business in a planned manner and not in unplanned manner so plan the business strategy before entering any business and then start.

CHAPTER 2

RESEARCH

Researching before starting your business is most important and the researching can be done with the following ways:

SURVEYS, STUDIES, ANALYSES, AND ASSESMENT

SURVERYS: Surveys are an essential element to start any business and it is very important to devote your good amount of time doing survey of how your business will do in the area where you would be starting your business. The Survey should be conducted with the target audience who would be the end user of the product which you would be giving it to the end user. The survey will also help you to analyse who your target audience would be and the approach which you would be doing will be a focused or targeted approached directly targeting the customers which your starting the business for instead of a random approach. The Survey mechanism also helps you to understand whether your business as compared to the competitors is different and whether you are using a different approach or can alter the product to satisfy the needs of the people you are targeting. There are various surveys mechanism which you can use like there are online surveys, taking physical surveys on printed forms in malls, stations etc where you can find the target audience. This will help you understand in a better way how your business will be doing in a longer run and since your business initially a local level it is very much important that you carry out survey before starting a business. The survey will also help you in understanding how to price your product or services as you will come to know directly from the survey what the target audiences are thinking about the business which you are starting.

STUDIES: As to start any business the study of the business is very important in your business it is also very much important that you carry out deeply the study of each and every factor about the business which your starting by spending time where similar kind of businesses are located or meeting the people and taking experiences from them about how the business is and what are the challenges they are facing and about how the business is in general. Once you thoroughly study about the business which you are starting you will come to know how feasible is the business and how to find the right approach to start your business in your locality. The studies about the business you can also do it by online research and studying about blogs of various materials which are online related to your business. The study of the business is the most important factor about starting the business and it will help you to take a logical approach on how to start your business. If the study involves in reading some books and to be able to start you can might as well get thru your friends or invest a little amount and buy the book before you start the business. There are several books and definitely you will find some books which are related to your business it is not at all a waste of time to go thru the books and read those as at the end of the day even if you don't start the business at least you will gain some knowledge about the said business. The study part also enables you to study on what all resources you would require to start your business.

ANALYSIS: Analyzing part comes once you have done the survey and study on the business which you are going to start. The data which you have collected needs to analyze in a proper way and time needs to be devoted for the same, the data collected will be a crucial one to make your business a successful one and analyzing the same will ensure that you will be in the market for a longer time. Once you get the data about the surveys which you have done you need to arrange them according to age, gender, income and occupation, now based on the business which you are starting you will come to know what percentage of people you will be able to target once you start the business and what is the percentage of expected income you would be able to generate once you start the business. The data collected from the studies about the business which you have done can be arranged in similar way the studies which have done should be in parts or sections and each sections should be dealing with various aspects of the business which you are starting. Like for example you are starting an online House Cleaning business services then you have to divide your study on how much people are there in your locality, study based on the effective and competitive cleaning material, study based on the casual labors to be used in the cleaning service, where to find such laborers, training part of the laborers, pricing of the services and payments terms etc. Overall analysis part is once you collect all the data pertaining to your business then you can have calculated approach and you are ready to launch your business. These are the main factors which can make or break your business so doing surveys, studies and analysis of those surveys, studies plays a crucial part in your business. This is the most tiring part but once done gives longer results.

ASSESSMENT

Assessment is nothing but self-analysis after studying doing survey and analyzing the data which you get from your business self-assessment is the most important think which you need to do, here assessment is done of whether you have a great idea or a great product and whether you have a product or an idea which will useful for a community. Once these assessments are carried out whether you have sufficient time to devote to successfully run your business and don't give up on it due to lack of time, whether you are professionally making a right choice and not doing something which will hamper your daily income source. The business assessments is very much important as in this you make a crucial decision of whether you want to do it part time or you have to do it full time by utilizing all your potential and time. The assessment can be done at your level and I can give you only ideas on how to go about doing an assessments finally coming to the conclusion after doing the assessment is totally your call, once you have done with the assessment you can start the business in your spare time or full time. If you feel you cannot let go your full time job I would always suggest you to start the business part time as you cannot let go your financial liabilities which you have. Nevertheless these kinds of assessments are very much important aspect and part of starting a business.

CHAPTER 3

PLANNING

Even though your business is small and without any investment, Planning of a business is an important aspect before starting any business. Once the identifying part is done Planning to start plays a major important role in starting of a business a business started in an unplanned manner not only suffers losses but a causes a major setback and can demotivate you leading to frustration and stress. The idea behind writing this book is to give you a step by step guidance on how not to get demotivated and give up. Step by Step planning of running a business will ensure durability and lesser chances of creating a panic situation if you already have a backup plan in place for any kind of problems which you would be facing in future, the business will not incurred loss or unsatisfied clients. Like for example planning a simple online coaching business you need a good computer, audio visual equipment's or a good configuration laptop, further soft wares like word and pdf converter to send assignments to your students, online video chatting software etc., once these planning is done you have schedule the time suitable and plan your day accordingly for the students to come online so that you deliver lectures to them. The Planning should be so seamless that there should be fewer margins of errors and the output would be as you desired. The Planning of the business makes you more focus on your main output and delivery system so that chances of facing setbacks are less. Plan in such a way that every minute details of starting up of your business is been taken care off. Anticipate on what all possible problems you might face in running your business make a note of it and ensure that all the possible solutions to cover up those problems are been taken care of.

An efficient planning to successfully run your business involves three major factors there may be many but 3 are the most important part in planning of a business.

- Before Starting of Business
- Executing
- Delivery

Before starting any business the initial preparation of organizing the things required to initially start the business. In this case when we are talking about the business where there are no investment starting or organizing things which are in your capacity which you can get without any monetary investment, like say for example you're starting a business of Freelance writing then going to free library getting free eBooks online for free references asking your friends and relatives whether they have any books which you are searching for, make sure you have a good laptop or desktop in your house for putting down whatever you write. Some free soft wares for correcting your grammars like grammerly.com and other website handy to ensure that there delivery of your writing is not hampered. If for example you are starting an event planning business then making sure you ties up with DJ, Party material supply stores or catering people and have as many options ready with you so that once you get the party order you have plenty of options to choose from for executing the event and then market you are business online.

Executing: Executing is the main part of planning a business and if the execution part is not been planned well is advance the whole idea of planning a business will be redundant. This part your business planning should take involves your maximum amount of time and needs to be properly carved out. The whole of idea of planning an execution of your business delivery is that there should be smooth flow of your business and without any hiccups or hindrances. In case of any kind of stoppages there should be a backup plan in place to cover up the stoppages or hindrances of the execution process. Even though your business is a simple home business still executing plays a major role in customer satisfaction and these are the customer who would recommend you in your initial phase to grow your business bigger.

Delivery: Delivery again has major importance in planning of a business and once you delivery the output you desire as per your planning the sense of satisfaction is tremendous which cannot be calculated in terms of any kind of monetary happiness. The Delivery as planned in timely manner is the most important for success of your business and thru which you come to know whether the planning which you have done has given you the expected resulted as you calculated. Delivering or giving the desire output as planned will decide whether you planning were successful or it needs to corrected or changed. As far as changing is concern the whole business planning is changing process and it keeps of changing or altering to the needs of your clients. To attain a perfect delivery mechanism it needs to have timelines, which can be calculated based on the time required for each and every activities involved in the business. The time can be divided into various aspects of your business execution to decide the delivery of your business. Say for example you are planning to start a simple business of Baking Cakes at home the time require to procure the items from the store the preparation time based on the oven you have and the number of people working on the baking process is involve needs to be calculated. Each and every task involved in the baking of cakes process needs to separated and time consumed for that very task needs to be calculated in order for giving time to clients and deciding the delivery of your product.

Likewise in any business all these three factors play a major role in planning of running any business, if your business is running in a planned even though small can reach high and scales which are unimaginable. There are many examples in our day to day life that small business has become big in a very short span of time if it involves dedication and right approach in a planned manner.

OBSTACLES

The Planning also includes planning of problem obstacles you might face before starting your business and during the business operations.

SETTING UP GOALS:

Setting up Realistic goals is very important for your business or anything for that matter is important as it will give you a definite direction on where to go and what to achieve. Working on any business model without goal is meaning less as if you do not achieve your ultimate aim of your business you might be demotivated. The Goals can be of Short Term Goals and Long Term Goals.

Short Term Goals – Short Term Goals can be of involving smaller task of setting up your business and time framing those shorter tasks in order to complete those goals on time. These fulfillments of short team goal will help to achieve the larger goal which you have targeted.

Long Term Goals – Long Term Goals again are those goals which will follow your shorter goals and ultimately will lead you to achieve the ultimate aim which you have decided to achieve in your business.

CHAPTER 4

CUSTOMER BASE

Once you are done with the Research and the Planning part the next thing to do is to generate a pre customer base before starting your business. You can use various methods to generate a Customer Base prior to start of your business like giving discounted launch offers, signup offers and extra services or products on signing up. Creating a customer base before starting up of your business will give you a head start and will make sure you have enough finances to carry out the business for a longer time. Money is the biggest motivator and if you are getting money beforehand even without starting the business will be a great motivator for you to start the business and sustain in the business for a longer time. This customer base is also important for you to create and these people would be your man source of income as they would be repeatedly come to you to buy your product or services. You have to use your survey forms and identify the customers which can be in group of your customer base. This customer would be your main target customer which you don't want to lose at any cost and they will ensure that your business will run for a longer time. You have to keep on increasing your customer base and never forget your loyal customer base. With surveys which you carry out you can also identify your customer based on which are your Potential Customers, Immediate Customers, Loyal Customers and Ignorant Customers

Potential Customers: These are those customers who are already using similar kind of products or services and are your potential clients, you always need to keep this customer hand and approach them every now and then to increase your customer base. These customers are those customers who can get switch over to your business immediately if given a good deal or offer. You have to make sure that you repeatedly connect with them and ask them about the services which they are using and how satisfy they are you can also connect with them by sending them offer and discount emails which can help these potential customers become your clients. The customers are the most care you need to take them and you need to be transparent about your business while dealing with them you have to always keep open yourself about any kind of doubt these customer has in your product or services. You have to always show these customers what the value of your product or services is and why it is important for them to join you. These customers even though they are doesn't immediately require your business or services they can require it later on so you have to never lose hope on these kinds of customer or client base.

Immediate Customers: Immediate customers are again those customers who are eagerly waiting to buy your product or services provided they get a good offer. The approach to these customers should be direct and if there is any kind of miscommunication it needs to be clear out immediately. The important thing is to make way for these customers to offer your product and services you can understand these kinds of customers from the survey form data analysis and once you identify these customers you can directly approach them for your product or services. To survive in the business targeting these customers is important as it will take care of your finances and the time and efforts which you are putting in the business. Even though if you have to make any alteration or reduce your cost in your product or services you have to make sure that these customers are not left and they are using your product or services.

Loyal Customers: Loyal customers are those people who like you and the business which your doing because of which they stick around with you for the services or products which you are giving to them. Never take these kinds of customer lightly and make sure you keep them happy by sending thank you notes or rewarding them for been a loyal customer. The most important factor is give them what you have promised or committed and never give false commitments to them, resolve their problems which they have with your services or products at the earliest make sure if you think give replacements like in example or bakery services replacing a cake which they didn't like this will not only create a stronger bond between you and customer but also help you to promote your business. You also have to ensure that you make your available for these kinds of customer as they will never leave you for anything. You also have to ensure to maintain credibility with these kinds of customer base in order to build a stronger trust for a longer term business relationship. There are also many great ways to thank loyal customers like giving them discounts on their birthdays and anniversaries sending them birthday cards with discounted offers or sending text messages of birthdays with discounted offer etc. My idea is that once you categorize the customer you know where to market the business to which customer and how to sustain your business and to grow your business.

Ignorant Customers: These are those customer base who are unaware or not educated customer about the product and services you are offering and are also not aware about the benefits which they will get if they take your product or services. You need to identify these customers and make them understand the products or services which you are offering in order for them to take your products or services. These ignorant customers may be ignorant in many different aspects and after taking one to one discussion about your business model and the things which you are giving in your business they will come to know what and how you are offering and how they can be benefited if they use your products or services. The ignorance may also be whether they are really requiring your products or services or it may be the risk factor which they are unable to take when they opt for your products or services. Nevertheless since you are best preacher of your business to turn these ignorant customers into potential customers is in your hands and you can better guide or educate these customers to take the right decision and generate lead based on your exchanges.

CHAPTER 5

QUALITY

The most important and crucial factor or any business is the quality or the product or services which they offer, a value for money offer will bring you repeated customers and if your giving good quality of products or services the customer is bound to come again to you. The quality of the products or services which you are offering therefore makes a crucial role in the business which you are doing. Please ensure you give your best and make optimum quality of products or services which you are offering. The end products or services your business portrays how well you have invested time in planning and research work in delivering those products or services. If you have not done any planning or research work in your products or services it shows in the end results, so by doing a business is a step by step process way the get an end result that is the quality of a great product or services depends upon the various factors.

Builds Trusts

Many believe that businesses won't succeed if they can't build customer trust. Countless potential sales are lost because a brand fails to make a deeper connection with prospective buyers. When you gain the confidence and loyalty of consumers, you're able to do more with your business, such as raise prices. The quality of your services and merchandise is one way to help you get consumers to appreciate and believe in what you have to offer. To connect with the customer is most important to way to connect with the customer can be identified by eyeing small details which are not easily visible or understandable. Once you connect with your customer it will become a long term business relationship of you and your customers. Customer trust with your products or services comes with your continues effort of giving quality product to them, once the trust is build up the customer will not leave your products or services at any cost.

Spreading the News

Customers trust brings you more customers as they market your products or services thru word of Mouth, please ensure that these customer also leave review your Facebook page and on the other social media platforms wherever you are marketing your products or services, this will enable you to increase your business giving an edge to you from your competitors. People when buying or taking any products or taking any kind of services takes recommendations from others and this is where your customer trusts comes into the picture. A customer having trust in your products or services will blindly recommend your product because of the faith and the trust the customer is having in your products or services.

Customer Complaints

The superior quality is also essential so that you get less customer complaints and more satisfied customers, this is will also ensures that the customer will come back and purchase your products and services repeatedly. A good service from a restaurant definitely differentiate them from other restaurant even though the food might not taste good, you would never want to go back to a restaurant where you have been mistreated and will always remember the service which you got. Similarly a good quality product or service will create a picture of your business in the customers mind and it is the impression which the customer carries after taking your products and services. It is therefore primarily most important that you work on the quality of the products or services and make sure that the efforts that you put in shows in the end products or the services.

Good Returns and Income

If you have a good quality products and services then you can always demand a premium price for the same once you get a good hold in the market of your business. This is what a proper research, planning and quality can do to the products and services which you are offering. The quality will speak for your products and services which you are offering enabling you to get more returns initially at the early stage itself, getting more returns and generating more income will enable you to put in more ideas as the finances of running the business which of prime importance is been taken care of. The income generated through the business will give you more confidence which will help you to sustain longer in the business without giving up.

CHAPTER 6

LEGAL

The business you would be starting would be legal that is a foolish question to ask, the business even though legal there are minute legal aspects of any business which you need to take care before starting any business. For example if you are starting a business of blogging or content developer making sure the content use is copy write free and it is your own idea which you are putting in the contents which you are using. There are similar smaller aspects like using you are own house commercially if you are starting some sales business as there are some rules and regulations using you are resident premises commercially. Other legal aspects would be if you require any kind of licenses the procurement of those licenses to start the business a business account to take the payments which you get from your clients. If you are doing it in a part time basis without leaving your job you need to use you are family members like you are non-working wife or mother make her the company owner and open an account in her name. This is important as for the part timers in most of the company's appointment letter, taking up or doing any part time employment or a business is prohibited and if it found that you are doing such a thing you might get terminated from the employment. Such kind of legal things you need to take care and then proceed with your business taking online payments or having legal company name is good for the business as the people rely on such business and they know that whatever money they are paying is safe and they are going to get the products or services what is promised. If you are entering into a contract or agreement with any company make sure you read and completely understand the contract or the agreement before signing it and alter the same if there are any clauses which you are not comfortable with. It is very important that you register your business even though small as that will enable to you to claim the intellectual property you have made by using the business. The registration of the business initially may not be important initially when you start but if the business is growing you have to register the business in a way your business will get a unique name and the name is essential to grow your business bigger. The business here I am talking about is a sole proprietorship business a single person business and no partners involve. However if you feel that a partner is require to initially start your business you can do it and it all depends on how you want to start your business. Starting a partnership business a simple Notarized partnership deed initially will suffice your need to start your small business at initial phase. Legally strong your business is it will safe guard you from any kind of financial losses as well as legal issues, try and make sure that you commit customer what is legally possible and not giving any fake or false commitments it will not only put into you into legal issues but will also hamper your business in turn spoiling your name in the market.

Legal expression even though sounds so heavy in initial phase of your home simple business should be taken in a subtle way and not to completely follow the legal implications as it possible that it might kill the very idea of you doing a business and we don't want that to happen. I am discussing about this topic in this book just because if there are any legal obligations which you require to fulfil in order to start your business you need to fulfil those to ensure that later on you won't face any hindrances in your business.

CHAPTER 7

TEAMWORK

Even though your business is a small and is single person operated business the teamwork I am talking about is the small people who are in background or invisible that makes to run your business smoothly. You don't have to forget about these people and make sure you build a strong team that will ensure smooth running of your business. For example the grocery supplier for your bakery business the internet service provider for your online business other small key players which enable you that you successful run your small business. The idea is that you make a strong reliable team which will help you in longer running of your business and to make it a successful one. To build a good strong team you have to identify good team players the players who are strong and reliable and are expert in their own field if they are not expert then you need to train them to become expert. Sometimes a team player with good dedication and ability to learn makes himself better from the other team players so might have to give an opportunity to such individuals who are keen in learning and making a small contribution in your business. Teamwork is also essential as it makes you run your business even if you are not available sometime; if you have a team in place as backup who can work on behalf of you that will take care of your business even if you are unavailable due to some commitments. The question now arises whether the team you are relying on will give same efforts in the business which you are giving that's when choosing of team players comes in, and if you have chosen right team players your job will be done even if you are unavailable. The team players as they are performing and doing their task assigned to them in your small home business ensure that they are compensated rightly for their work, no matter how much share they get in your business it will keep their motivation boosted and making them more and more reliable for you to carry out their task. The compensation also should be given to them at the right time in order to keep them going if you are only selfishly taking all the fruits of the business without considering their efforts then very good chance is that you will lose your team players and your idea making the business big will be a far vision. Single headedly you can take your business to a limited market but with a team you can target a larger market as you get many more hands to help you with your business in the same amount of time. You can involve your family members as well to become your team players as it will also help you to get reliable team players with stronger association. You can learn the benefits of team work in any team game if as a team gives an equal efforts and everybody performs on the field the team is definitely going to outperform the team which has not performed as a team. Building up a team you need to ensure that you support your team members and help them to become like you and not to take mistakes in small things or errors they do.

DELEGATION OF WORK

This again a very important aspect of the business which you need to do in order for you to concentrate on crucial aspects of the business and the area which requires you maximum time in order for your business to grow, all other non-essential tasks can be delegated to other people or team players which will help you to give maximum time in your business to the main task for which you are solely responsible and dependent in order for you to make sure the business is running. This again depends upon business to business and once you have done proper planning of the business you will come to know which are the non-essentials tasks which you need to delegate in order for you to focus on your main business. Delegation of work which is non-essential when the quantum of business you are getting is more so to prepare for the future you might as well have to start early and to prepare a team where you can divert the non-essential task of your work to some other. The key here is once you delegate the non-essential task of your business to other you can focus on the most important part of your business and get more to time to innovate and get more ideas into the business helping your business to grow.

Delegated non-essential part of your business will help to sustain longer and focus on your main task instead of getting burn out and completely exhausted by doing all the task all alone. Once you get this thing in place you will see that your business is flourishing with more and more clients as you keep on focusing on the main part of your business. There are various elements of delegation of task or work which you do

Specific: you need to be specific on what kind of task you have to delegate so that very amount of work you can delegate and ensure that the specific task is only done making it simpler for you to quantify the time require and the amount of work that can be delegated.

Measurable: the delegated task assigned must be measurable to ensure that you compensate them is a good way so that further the individual can be utilize for similar task or any other task as per the requirement of your business.

Agreed: Ensuring that the task which you are assigning to the individual is agreeable, and that individual is ready to deliver the task in the way which you wanted. If there is any training requirement to fulfil those task you need to understand and ensure that the relevant training is provided in order for the individual to complete the task.

Realistic: once agreed making sure it is realistic time and task is given so that the individual fulfill those task in the time assigned to him, realistic goal setting is really important for the individual to fulfill the task in a timely manner.

The delegation part I am discussing because initially it may be that you are able to carry out your business without help from anyone but as the business grows you need to ensure that this delegation of work is essential to keep your business growing with the growing number of clients. The non-essential parts of your business anyways are those parts where you don't require much of your attention and can be done without your supervision. Identifying these non-essential parts in your business is of most important for that planning is essential which I have discuss in my earlier chapter in this book. Once you delegate a part of your work and instructed the individual by showing him how to perform that part by giving him clear cut guidelines or explaining him the process of how it is done you can always with your minimum supervision can ensure that the task will be done at the end if at all you require some minimum alteration of correction that's justifiable as you have saved your crucial time which otherwise would have got wasted in doing this non-essential tasks.

CHAPTER 8

OBSTACLES, COMPETITORS AND TIME

There is no work which has some or the other obstacles and to overcome these obstacles is necessary so that you focus on the business which you want to do.

Mental Obstacles – Mental Obstacles are the major road blocks for your business.

Failure of Fear – Fear of getting failure is the greatest obstacle which will stop you in starting your business and it is of prime importance to remove all the fear and take the risk of starting the business.

Lack of Direction – Lack of direction is the another obstacle and without direction of what to do an what not apprehends you to stop from starting anything new or doing something which your family will not support.

COMPETITIORS

Competitors at the initial stage of your simple small business is not so important as your business will be at the local stage and you will be at the early stage of your business, but knowing your competitors is prime important as it will help you in the business which you would be doing. It is very important for you to know the competitors what products and services they are offering and what different you can do to stand out from your competitors. To know about the competitors business and their pricing of the products or the services is prime important to know in order for you to offer your products or services at competitive prices. To studying about the competitors and their weakness will enable you to gain an edge over them and get their unsatisfied client in your business.

To know about your competitors and how they are catering their customer you can might as well use their services and see how they are operating there businesses. This is good way in learning about your competitors, like what type of products or services they are offering, how they are targeting the customers and what all things they are doing for running their business. The other options to know about your competitors is to check online whether there are any reviews articles or feedback about your competitors business which you can refer and know about your competitor.

If your competitors have any websites you can check the information of your competitor on their websites and also can see what all products and services they are offering. You can also find the competitors of your business by using search engines and on Google you can find who locally your competitors are, you do more research on them by asking for their pamphlets and various other information like their price list etc. This will give a fair idea on how they are treating their customers how much discounts they are offering and how competitive they are in the market.

Knowing about you competitors will also help you to understand the potential of your business in the market which you are offering and how the customers are reacting to the business been offered to them. Once you have gather all the information you require about your competitors it is very important for you to understand the information collected and analysing it so that you can do better than your competitors. There is good chance that the information you have collected of your competitors can give you a loop hole of his business and the drawbacks in his business which you can cover up and will safe guard you from doing the same mistakes in your business.

This information which you have collected will also give you a fair idea to you on how you can alter your business plan to suit the requirements of your customers. It is of prime importance that you try and input your creativity, ideas in your business and not to copy the business model of your competitor.

Try and innovate as much as possible in your business idea people like creativity and innovation is key to the success of your business.

TIME

There is an important saying that you have to become a master of time and not salve. Managing time is an important aspect of any business and if you are able to efficiently manage your time then you can get maximum output from your business with minimum effort. Respecting and valuing time is very important part of your business as it decides on how to achieve your goal by valuing time which is there in your hand as once the time is gone it never comes back.

Time is the essential element of your business, time to decide when to launch the product and timely delivery of the product is crucial to achieve your business goals.

CHAPTER 9

SOME SIMPLE SMALL BUSINESS IDEAS TO START FROM YOUR HOME

After discussing in length about how to start your simple home business I would like to share with you some of simple home business ideas which you can use it and start your simple home business with minimum or low investments. I really cannot say zero investment as you are investing your crucial time and efforts which cannot calculate in terms of money so there is an investment. Even if you do not get succeeded at least you have learned something and once you get the taste of doing something on your own you are bound to start again as there is famous quote from Steve Jobs "it is impossible to fail if you learn from your mistakes and don't give up" life is all about mistakes and learning from those mistakes never giving up on the dreams you always thought of the 09:00 to 05:00 job which you are doing might not give you so much learning as you would be getting when you start on your own by doing small simple business at your home. Trust me once you start any kind of small home business you will identify the true potential in yourself, and once you get into the self-survival mode nothing will stop you from turning back.

I am sharing some small home business ideas which will be helpful in your journey of starting up of small business from your home, these business ideas you might be aware of and some of you must also had it in your mind but I am sharing these some of the ideas just because you can get fair idea of how to start your small home business and some of you can relate yourself with the business ideas which I am sharing

Day or Child Caring Services

These are mostly related to the people who have their own children even if you don't have children some of you can take up small course or read book about child care services and start this simple small business from your home. If you already have a child or parented a child you are experience in this field and that is a great advantage you have to start the business. Day care business now a days is the need of hour as more and more parents opting for the same as both are working parents the cost of living has increased with increase in the daily expenses of the family so both the parents now a days are working and day care services for their children becoming an essential service requirement. You can start this business online by marketing it on Facebook, whatsapp or any other social media platforms which you want to market it to your friends and family members and getting your customers from there.

Blogging

This is again a great simple business idea to start from your home, you can do this in your leisure time and comfort of your home the blogging can be on a blogging website or a making video blogs on YouTube. You have a team to get content for your blog or you can choose a subject of your choice for creating a blog. The blog can be anything right from an tour to any place with your friends a restaurant outing, giving details about how was the food what to eat in a travel blog you can write or do video on how to go to the place and the things to explore there what are cost of the travel you incurred and various other stuff like that, if you are expert in some subjects you can write about that in the blog or make videos. Blogging is a great way to display your talents if you have any, a details blogs made on anything which has smaller details which cannot find anywhere on the internet a great way to make your blog successful. The blogging which you will create will generate income for you by the traffic it generates by the people visiting the blog so it is very important for you to share your blog online on your Facebook, Instagram, WhatsApp and other social media platforms. Successful bloggers often get invites from good companies to write reviews about their products or services and are paid a good amount for the services which they offer.

Freelance Writing

This is another very lucrative small business idea which you can from your home, nowadays many companies requires freelance writers to write about their products or services which they offer and this is where the freelance writers comes into the picture, if you are good at writing about something you might as well use this business option. Publication houses also hire Freelance writers to write about something on their blog where there are numerous followers to the blog there are various products and services which a company manufactures and Freelance writers are require writing the manuals and other scripts about how to use their products and services. There are content writing for websites for which freelance writers are been hired again to market your abilities you have use online social media platforms and show them that you are available as freelance writer to take up jobs there also social media platforms which offer such kinds of part time jobs which you can apply.

Event Planning

Event planner for a small house parties or parties in a society is a good simple house business which you do it part time and if you are good at planning parties and a party animal who likes to party you might as well try this business opportunity a good event planner is always been approaches and if you have good contacts you will get good amount of business in this field. Small parties and small corporate events arranging catering, sounds and lights for such events has become common scenario and event planning has become prime importance and if you have good planning skills and know how to plan events then you can chose this business as an option to start your small business. Again you have to get to social media platforms also approach some of your local hotels, banquet halls and associate with them in order for you to get business. You can also tell your friends and relatives about your business and offer your services at discounted rates, similarly also tell them to promote you and to give genuine feedbacks about your services.

Social Media Management

This is very great and lucrative field and these kind of business has been come up recently, it a very crucial task and to manage someone's social media page or account has become the most important thing in today's world. A good updated social media account is needed for people so that the followers to their page increases and people doesn't know how to manage that, where your skills of managing a social media page for them would be useful and you can use this skills to manage their social media accounts. For this you need to be good in some skills which you can easily acquire by learning it from someone who already does and manages accounts for someone else. This business has very good potential and requires basic knowledge of using social media platforms like uploading their photos writing the messages which they need to give through social media. The business has huge potential and if you are successful in doing this business it will generate good amount of income for you at the leisure of your home. Initial to get business you have to market yourself online as well as use some of your contacts to get some of the clients to start off, once you have some successful clients you can charge your new client's good amount of money for managing their social media accounts. Once you gain skills of managing their account you can also give tips on how to increase their followers and how to get more content which they can put and charge them for the advices which you are giving.

Virtual Assistance

This is a kind of business which is newly started in this you manages a company's clients and take manage appointments for some of the companies manager at the leisure of your home, it is like managing the calendar of the managers working for a particular company and set meetings for them looking at their schedule, and if the meetings are overlapping rescheduling them, and giving them a new slot, it is just like working as a personal assistance for a company from home. This business is like an organizer who is assisting a company to run smoothly and to stay their company organized by working on the schedules and task in timely manner, it is also a business of managing their communications and cutting the cost of the employees which they require for doing such task or job.

Handmade Product Sales

Handmade decorative products from waste or paintings can be made and sold on the online E commerce platforms; nowadays many people are buying stuff online and looking for different kinds of artworks online a cheaper price to decorate their home. These people are also looking for some unique items which are attractive which can be used to decorate their homes. Paintings were and will always be the best things to do and sell online if you are good at paintings you might as well try this business opportunity for this you have to initial market your products on free social media platforms like olx or quikr or on Facebook or Whatapp once you have good order you can always chose to start an online store on Amazon to start selling your products. You can always develop your skills and learn various ways of how to make good hand made products online thru YouTube or any other platforms to make new items and grow your simple small home business.

Ecommerce Reselling

This is like buying it from someone and selling it to the other you personally are not involve in manufacturing of the product but you have good contacts with the person who can source you the product and you have a readymade customer base to sell those products. You can readily use this opportunity and start the simple small home business of reselling and make this opportunity at good use. This you just have to do some set up of how to manage on work on how deliver the goods take your commission out of the payments which you receive.

Second-hand Store

This is very good business opportunity where you can set up a second hand store items in your house or online also you can sell these second hand items you can purchase these items from someone at a very low price and sell them by keep some profit. You can put up a store in your basement parking or in your society once a week to sell items from your second hand store you can also use online platforms like Facebook and WhatApp to market these products.

Bakery

Some individuals have excellent baking skills and because of these they can think bakery business as an option to start there simple home business, you can distribute leaflets in the newspapers in your nearby area and do advertising of your bakery business. You can also market about your bakery products by doing tie ups with hotels and banquet hall nearby. You can also tie up with the catering service providers for supply of cakes to them and grow your customer base. There is good business opportunities for providing customises cakes which you can learn and provide customise cakes and bakery items to your customers. A good homemade cake is where many people nowadays opt for as they know that the cake is homemade and hygienic, this gives a good opportunity for you to sell your bakery items as in current scenario individuals are ready to pay a premium price for good quality and hygienic products. Lastly you can always use social media platforms like Facebook, WhatApp etc to market your products to your friends and family members.

Catering Services

Starting a small catering business from home and taking small party orders of 100 – 150 people can be done from home and doesn't require big set up of utensil and other equipment's. The customers nowadays opt for homemade hygienic health food and the homes made catering as well as tiffin services are making good business in the market today. There many people who are successfully running the business for years and making good money out of it as we all are aware food is a daily requirement and without food no one can live. The food business is the only business which has good profit margins. Starting this business you can advertise locally on social media platforms and tying up with some small event management companies who manage small events. Online also thru various social media platforms you can market about your services.

Event Photography or Photography

A good or professional Photographer in today's world earns good amount of money, you can be an event photographer or a freelance photographer taking pictures which you like. There are many individuals who has hobby of photography as a photographer it is very important for you to have a good Instagram profile to portray your work. Nowadays freelance photographers take any random models in shopping malls and take their pictures to portray their work on their Instagram profile. They also get good amount of work in such a way some photographers goes to a particular location and click pictures and portray there work there are many different ways to build up these business. The main idea is to get a good amount of your work to make it online. Photographer is also a good editor and it is very important part of photography. This also mostly you have to market about this business online on the social media platforms.

Tutoring / Preparing Notes/Online Tutoring

Teaching profession can be a good source of income if you have good qualification and enjoy teaching, this good old business is flourishing nowadays and there are few quality tutor who are there which are really taking the profession in the real sense and giving right education which the students require, today the coaching centre have become a money making business. As good quality tutor you can definitely make a difference if you are good in teaching, you can do it at your home or you can start online tuitions for your students. You can also prepare notes of various subjects and can generate good amount of income from, students are always interested in easy to understand notes of any subjects and parents are ready to pay any amount for such well-prepared notes. You need to distribute leaflets in front of school and colleges as well as do some marketing online in order to get some students to start your simple home tutoring business. This is the profession which will not close down even if there is recession in the market and the only sector which has never shown downfall.

Proofreading or Editing or Checking

This simple small home business you can do at your flexible time and schedule and earn good income from the same. If you have good command in any language you can offer proofreading services to authors, book writers or content developers and earn good income. To find such jobs there are many such websites online where you can proofreading or editing jobs you also can market yourself by creating a good profile on the social media platforms.

Career Guidance/ International Education Consulting work

If you are good at following current market trends in the job sector you can might as well thing of starting a consulting business and consulting the students about which career to choose and guiding them in finding the best suitable career for them by providing them insight about the job industry. In the similar manner you can also start an international Education related consulting work where you can market the International Educational courses of International Colleges to students here in India and can earn great income with also additional perks of travelling abroad. To advertise this business you have to use social media platforms and visit colleges and school asking them for doing presentation on the career opportunities and offering your consultancy services to students. The source of income in this business is good and there are plenty of opportunities as good number of students often go abroad for their future studies. For this you can take up some courses or learn about it online on how to do career guidance and how to offer overseas educational opportunities to the students in India.

Resume Building Services

If you are experience in the corporate field and have experience in the field of human resources and recruitment you can start a small home business of Resume Building Services for job seekers. You can also help the job seekers with their covering letter and train them how to give job interviews. You can go to colleges and various institutes to market you services. There are many job seekers who are willing to pay for a good resume and this is where your expertise will help them to seek them job. This is good small home business which you can do at your convenient time and comfort of your home.

Gardening

This is the services where if you are good at setting up a garden you can help set up a garden for someone and if you know which plants to pick and how to maintain those plants you can start a simple small business to set up a garden for someone. This will include choosing right plants for them maintaining it regularly and guiding them on how to water them and take care of them. For marketing about your business you can use social media platforms like Facebook and WhatApp to offer your services.

Gift Service

Gifting is common scenario and most of the time people are confused about what to gift to someone. You can start a gift services small simple business by giving them ideas on what to gift and offer them gift baskets of variety of gift option from your catalogue and taking commission on the sale which you do. This business once you get a good client base you will be approached not only during festive seasons but also for special occasions. You need to keep yourself updated with latest gifting updates and prepare a catalogue accordingly. The gifts can be anything from electronic to gold ornaments to small things. You can marketing your gifting business to your friends and family members and your close associates initially to start off with and later on can market it in a bigger way once the business starts making profit.

Web Designing

Some of you might be good in Web Designing and can take up jobs as a freelancer which are been posted on various websites and do work for them. There are many small companies and start-ups that are looking for a freelance web designer for designing their website. Web Designer not only designs the website but maintains also for a monthly fixed compensation. You can also post your profile on the Social media platforms and market your skills as a web designer, you can tell your clients to promote your work and get more clients for you.

Graphic Designing

You can also offer graphic design services to those who need help making things like logos, marketing materials or other branding elements.

App Development

If you're skilled specifically with mobile technology, you can build a business designing apps for clients or even creating your own to sell in mobile marketplaces.

Group Activities

If you are good planner of any outdoor event like trekking, bike riding or anything which suits your interest you can start an activity based group and plan monthly activities of such groups, like going to trekking visiting any local travel destination. There are many individuals who are interested in joining such group activities and it is good source of income along with pursuing your hobby. There also people who organized sport various sport events and earn good profits from them. You make WhatApp group of people who are interested in joining your activity and accordingly you can post what kind of activities your planning so that interested people can join your activity group. These activities photos you can post on your social media accounts in order to help you to increase your business and your client base.

House or Office Cleaning Business

This business you can start off with your own small work force and in your local area can use this small work force and provide cleaning services every day or as and when require basis in your locality. In this you just have to take order and manage your cleaning staff to complete the order. This is very good lucrative businesses as there are many people who require cleaners to clean their premises. You need to market your business online as well as by distributing leaflets locally in shop and small offices where daily cleaning requirements are there and people are require daily to clean the offices.

Music Instruction

You can post online videos on YouTube and train people online on how to play Music Instruments if you are good at playing any kind of music instruments. There are many individuals who are keen on learning any music instruments but don't have time to travel and give time for such things. You can use this opportunity and make online classes available to them and can also take personalize coaching online to teach such people.

Clothing Design /Alteration

If you are good in altering cloths or designing any cloth you can start this simple small business from your home and design or alter cloths of people. It is very difficult to find good tailors who can design cloths you can help these people in designing their cloths and can even have an option of selling the design cloths online or have an in house store. People who wear such cloths are loyal to their tailors and never leave them for any other person. It is kind of creating a brand of yourself in your locality. You can use social media platforms to market your business and also can promote within your friends and family members.

Personal/Yoga Training

If you are good in Yoga or Physical fitness is your hobby then you might as well think of starting this business of giving personal training online thru social media platforms. This will help to create good secondary income for you as well as it will keep you more fit in the process. Personal trainers are in demand nowadays as there are more and more people due to awareness indulge in regular exercise and a right personal trainer to guide them properly to do reach their fitness goals is always in demand. You can market this business by giving free live sessions on Facebook and YouTube and then later on make the individuals who are joining your free sessions into permanent clients. You can also take help of your friends and family members in order to promote your business as well you can start a YouTube channel and post some fitness videos online to increase your client base.

Interior Decorating

Even though you are not a qualified home interior decorator and you enjoy designing and decorating home you can take this hobby of yours and make it as a business opportunity for generating business. You can take up small assignments of home as well small office decoration helping them giving ideas of which flooring to use, which wall paper will best suits the home or office and make good income with your consulting. You can also help your clients in finding good suitable vendors to source their material for interior decoration and making some commission out of it, you can also do tie ups with the flooring, wall paper vendors for giving best deals to your clients. To market this business you can do it online or get assistance with your friends and family members to get your initial clients. Once you have done work of few clients the clients themselves will promote your work to others. Interior designing and decoration is a continuous work and new market trends keep on coming so you have to keep up with the market trends which are going.

Affiliate Marketing

There are various e – commerce websites which allows you to become there partners and do affiliate marketing for them Amazon is one of them. If you share the links of their products on your Facebook profile or WhatsApp and if through those links people shop on Amazon, Amazon gives you commission based on that. This business many people does and generates has good income by doing Affiliate marketing. The good part of the business is that you can do it anytime and anywhere at your comfort.

Online Course Creation

If you have expertise in any particular field you can create course module of the same and market the same online. There are many different areas where there are special courses requirements, you have to be good in your presentation skill and might as well take up some small online free Word courses to prepare Power Point Presentation of your course module. You can use online platforms to market your courses and also approach institute or colleges where the courses offered by you can be used to the students.

Pickle, Masala and Papad Business

If you are good at making Pickle, homemade masala or papads this is very good lucrative business and can earn good profit in the business. You can market this business online and also do tie ups with the local stores in your area initially to start your business. As the customers develop taste for your items you can hire some staff and can start small scale business of the same.

Snacks business

Just like pickle, masala and papad business if you are good at making homemade snacks you can make the same and sell it at your local stores. There is very big market for homemade snacks. You can use online platform also to market your products apart from selling it to the local stores.

Apart from this there are many more small businesses which you can start with small amount of capita if you really want to start a second income and turned that into a full time business. I have read a good article on various business option on yourstory.com where the writer has given 20 different business ideas which you can start from home with small amount of capital, ranging from Handmade Candles, Agarbattis, Buttons, Designer Laces, Ice Cream Cones and many more you can learn more about such business in detail on the website, where you can get various small business ideas and how to start the same given by the writer online.

INVESTING TIME ON SOCIAL MEDIA

All these business ideas can be of our use and you can utilize these ideas for starting up your simple small business from your home. The other thing which you can do is simultaneously start your YouTube Channel and uploading your business journey in order to inspire it to other people to start their own businesses. The starting of YouTube channel will not only promote your business but will also generate small amount of income from the channel. The YouTube Channel will also promote you as a brand and today brand value or image creation has become prime importance. It is most important that before the start of your business and while doing your business you invest considerable time on social media platforms and take maximum use of these platforms as it is free and today everybody is online and all these platform has become day to day activity and to visit once there Facebook account check what is there on WhatsApp has become an integral part of our life.

Google – Google also gives lots of option of listing your local business online Nowadays people use Google search engines to check for each and everything even there are small businesses you will find it on Google, make sure you use this platform extensively and list your business on Google. The Google also provides you to put small description of your product in the search and also gives you an option to give link to your website leading to your business. The Google searches also have customer's reviews on it which is very important to grow your small business. This review definitely makes difference when the customer decides to opt for your products or services.

Branding Yourself: Investing time on social media platform is basically to create yourself as a brand, you need to brand yourself and the business which you are doing will automatically follow, there is famous quote from the Facebook inventor – Mark Zuckerberg *"Think about what people are doing on Facebook today. They're keeping up with their friends and family, but they're also building an image and identity for themselves, which in a sense is their brand".*

This is what you have to do with yourself and build an image or a brand which will speak for your product itself even if locally people should identify you and then the product or business which you are offering. Therefore many people named their business on their very own names.

CHAPTER 10

SUCCESS STORIES

There are many people who have been successful in making simple small home business and have achieve great leaps and bound and I am sharing some success stories of small business ideas

The Handmade Apparel and Accessories business brand named Lavish this brand is not so old but the owner Aarushi in 2017 and today the brand has market share value of over Rs 20 lakhs, the brand was started at home with a very small investment of Rs 30,000/- the passion for making handmade accessories made the young entrepreneur to sell her products locally and then on Amazon. Today the brand is exporting this made in India accessories to US, Italy , Denmark and various other parts of the world. This small business of her was started as part time and not it has become a full time business earning good amount profit from the business. This is a great example of how a passion can turn into a full time business for you and to reach leaps and bound which you have never imagined. (Ref: yourstory.com)

Another very young entrepreneur story I would like to quote here is of the product name Oziva started by Aarti Gill, Oziva is an Indian company and no.1 nutrition brand and currently is a 50 Crore brand company. (Ref: yourstory.com)

I would also like to share story of Japna Rishi Kaushik and her health snack brand Hungry Foal which she started from a small room from her home, to fight the increasing number of malnutrition cases among children's. She started the company with her husband in the year 2016, by using good research strategy and studying the market before launching her product. She priced her product as low as Rs 5 and Rs 10 readily making it available in local kirana stores so that the children buy these health snacks and get free from malnutrition. While starting this company she did not thought that the company would make an profit of Rs 3.6 Crore annually. (Ref: yourstory.com)

All these young entrepreneurs have proved that there is no barriers to the limitless ideas of mind which you utilize and power which you have within yourself and make your like a meaningful one. Each and every one of you who is reading this book has taken the first step in doing something on your own and that itself a big thing the next step is to implement the great idea which you have by following the simple steps which I have mentioned in this book to make your idea a big success and example like this above to follow.

ABOUT THE AUTHOR

Advocate Abhishek Gokhale is a practicing Criminal and Civil lawyer, also a degree holder of Masters in Business Administration. A Business Speaker, Small Business Project Consultant who has spent a considerable amount of time associating himself with big Corporate Firms and also was closely associated with the people who has created their big business from the scratch.